Japanese American Internment Camps

CORNERSTONES OF FREEDOM

SECOND SERIES

Gail Sakurai

Children's Press®
A Division of Scholastic Inc.
New York • Toronto • London • Auckland • Sydney
Mexico City • New Delhi • Hong Kong
Danbury, Connecticut

Photographs © 2002: AP/Wide World Photos: 39 (Damian Dovarganes), 30, 31, 33 (Julie Jacobson), 34; Corbis Images: 29, 45 bottom right (Nathan Benn), 5 bottom right, 6, 36, 44 right (Bettmann), 5 bottom left, 27 (Mariners' Museum), 37 (Wally McNamee), 4, 22 (UPI), 41 (Dean Wong), 11, 12, 26, 28, 44 left; Library of Congress: 3 background, 7, 21, 35; National Archives and Records Administration: 14 (Clem Albers/WRA), cover top, 45 top right, 13 (Dorothea Lange/WRA), 18 (Parker/WRA), 23 (Francis Stewart/WRA), cover bottom, 9, 15, 24, 32, 45 left.

XNR Productions: Maps on pages 15, 17

Library of Congress Cataloging-in-Publication Data

Sakurai, Gail.
    Japanese American internment camps / by Gail Sakurai.
       p. cm.—(Cornerstones of freedom. Second series)
    Includes bibliographical references (p.) and index.
    Summary: Discusses the mass relocation of thousands of Japanese Americans during World War II, profiling individuals such as Daniel Inouye, Yoshiko Uchida, and George Takei.
    ISBN 0-516-22276-7
    1.World War, 1939-1945—Concentration camps—United States—Juvenile. 2. Japanese Americans—Evacuation and relocation, 1942-1945—Juvenile literature. 3. World War, 1939-1945—Japanese Americans—Juvenile literature. [1. Japanese Americans—Evacuation and relocation, 1942-1945. 2. World War, 1939-1945—Japanese Americans.] I. Title. II. Series.
    D769.8.A6 S25 2002
    940.54'7273—dc21
                                                            2001003566

1 2 3 4 5 6 7 8 9 10 R 11 10 09 08 07 06 05 04 03 02

FRIGHTENED CHILDREN CLUTCHED their parents' hands. The adults were scared, too, but they tried hard not to show their fear. Armed soldiers herded the families onto the trains and buses that would carry them far away from their comfortable homes. The United States government was sending Japanese Americans to bleak prison camps. How had such a terrible thing come to pass?

★ ★ ★ ★

A massive amount of destruction occurred when Japanese planes bombed Pearl Harbor.

PEARL HARBOR

Just before eight o'clock on a bright Sunday morning, Japanese warplanes swooped from the sky bringing death and destruction to the United States territory of Hawaii. Seventeen-year-old Daniel Inouye was dressing for church when the radio blared, "The Japanese are bombing Pearl Harbor! This is not a drill!"

It was December 7, 1941, and Japan was bombing the American naval base at Pearl Harbor, near Honolulu, Hawaii. About one hundred ships were in the harbor at the time of the surprise attack. Twenty-one American ships were destroyed or severely damaged, and nearly two hundred planes at nearby airfields were destroyed on the ground. After a Japanese bomb hit its **ammunition** storeroom,

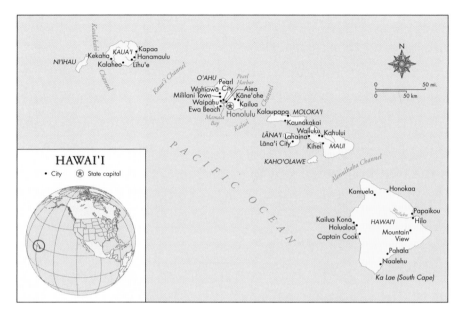

Map of Hawaii. Honolulu is marked by the red star on the island of O'ahu.

HAWAII

Hawaii is a chain of volcanic islands extending 1,523 miles (2,451 kilometers) across the central Pacific Ocean. It is made up of 8 major islands and 124 minor ones. Hawaii became the fiftieth state of the United States on August 21, 1959.

the battleship USS *Arizona* exploded and sank within nine minutes. Nearly 1,200 crewmembers of the *Arizona* were killed.

Daniel Inouye watched in horror from the yard of his family's Honolulu home as the Japanese planes dropped

The battleship USS *Arizona* at sea (left), and sinking in Pearl Harbor during the attack (right).

5

their deadly cargo. By the end of the brief attack, nearly 3,500 people were wounded or killed.

Americans were outraged by the unprovoked Japanese attack. Until that morning, the United States and Japan were not at war. In fact, the United States had been trying very hard to stay out of the war that was raging in Europe and Asia. Now Americans had no choice but to fight back. The following day, December 8, 1941, the United States declared war on Japan.

WAR HYSTERIA

After the attack on Pearl Harbor, Americans were angry and afraid. If Japanese planes could bomb Hawaii, they might also try to attack the West Coast of America. Many people directed their fear and anger at Americans of Japanese **ancestry.**

A newspaper headline from December 8, 1941

* * * *

A sign from a Japanese grocer declaring his allegiance to the United States

In 1941 there were about 160,000 Japanese Americans living in Hawaii. Another 125,000 Japanese Americans lived on the United States mainland, most of them on the West Coast. Two-thirds were U.S. citizens born in America, and all were loyal to the United States. But to other Americans, they looked like the enemy.

Many Americans were overcome by war **hysteria,** and were feeling an unreasoning hatred for anything Japanese, including their fellow Americans. People who had always been prejudiced against Japanese Americans suddenly felt justified in their hatred. Japanese Americans had done nothing wrong, but they shared a common ancestry with the enemy pilots who bombed Pearl Harbor.

In Hawaii there was little prejudice against Japanese Americans. On the mainland, however, a long-standing resentment had existed for forty years. Some people feared losing their jobs to Japanese immigrants, who were often willing to work for lower wages. Differences in language, customs, religion, and appearance also played a part in the prejudice against Japanese Americans.

Pressure from labor unions and special interest groups forced the government to pass restrictive and discriminatory laws against Japanese immigrants. In 1922 the Supreme Court ruled that Asian immigrants could not become U.S. citizens. (Their children who were born in the United States were automatically citizens.) In 1923 non-citizens were forbidden to own land, and in 1924, Congress halted any further Japanese immigration.

On the day Pearl Harbor was bombed, Yoshiko Uchida was a nineteen-year-old college senior at the University of California in Berkeley. She lived in a comfortable three-bedroom house in Berkeley with her parents and older sister, Keiko. That afternoon she returned home from studying for final exams at the campus library to find her world turned upside down.

LEGAL DISCRIMINATION

Takuji Yamashita came to the United States in 1893 at the age of eighteen. He learned English, went to college, and earned a law degree in 1902. He was not allowed to become a lawyer because he was not a U.S. citizen.

8

A notice for Japanese men to sign up for relocation

★ ★ ★ ★

GEORGE HOSHIDA

George Hoshida, a husband and the father of four daughters, was arrested and sent from his home in Hawaii to a prison camp on the mainland. The FBI claimed that Hoshida's leadership in the Buddhist church and his interest in judo made him "potentially dangerous" and "suspicious."

The FBI had searched the Uchida home and taken her father away for questioning. The family had no idea where Mr. Uchida was, what had happened to him, or when he would return. After five days they finally learned that Mr. Uchida and about one hundred other men had been arrested because they were leaders in the Japanese American community. A few days later, these men were sent to a prison camp in Montana. They had suddenly become "enemy **aliens**" because they were born Japanese.

Within a few weeks of the attack on Pearl Harbor, the government arrested and jailed without trial more than two thousand Japanese American men from Hawaii and the West Coast. Some were successful businessmen, like Mr. Uchida. Others were bankers, lawyers, journalists, teachers, farmers, and fishermen. No criminal charges were ever filed against them. Most of them were held in prison camps until the end of the war.

Japanese Americans had always been extremely patriotic and loyal to the United States, but that no longer seemed to matter. Years of anti–Japanese American prejudice erupted into outright hatred and suspicion. Many stores and restaurants refused to serve Japanese Americans. Some people called them by the deliberately hurtful term "Jap."

Wild rumors spread that Japanese Americans in Hawaii had helped guide the Japanese bomber pilots to their targets. All Japanese Americans were suspected of spying for Japan, without the slightest evidence. Newspapers published articles calling Japanese Americans "the enemy

＊ ＊ ＊ ＊

within." Despite these suspicions and accusations, there was never a single confirmed case of spying or **treason** by a Japanese American during World War II.

Military and political leaders joined in the hostility. They claimed that there was no way to tell which Japanese Americans were loyal and which were disloyal. They were all considered a threat to United States security.

EXECUTIVE ORDER 9066

On February 19, 1942, President Roosevelt signed Executive Order 9066. This order allowed military leaders to make any area in the United States into a restricted military zone for reasons of national defense. On March 2 the U.S. Army announced that the West Coast states of California, Oregon, Washington, and Arizona were a restricted military zone.

President Franklin D. Roosevelt, shown here signing the Declaration of War against Japan

⋆ ⋆ ⋆ ⋆

The army established curfews for all Japanese Americans in the restricted zone. They had to stay inside their houses between 8 P.M. and 6 A.M., and they were not allowed to travel more than five miles from home. They were ordered to turn in all weapons, cameras, binoculars, and shortwave radios, as these were considered tools for spies.

The army announced that Japanese Americans would soon be "excluded," or removed, from the restricted zone. Japanese Americans were encouraged to voluntarily leave the area. Most people had no place to go and could not easily leave their homes and jobs. By the end of March 1942, only a few thousand Japanese Americans had left the West Coast on their own. Voluntary **relocation** was canceled.

Japanese people packing up their belongings for relocation

* * * *

Children wearing their registration tags

Forced relocation of Japanese Americans from the West Coast began immediately. All persons of Japanese ancestry were ordered to report for registration and instructions. Each family was given a registration number. They received only a week to ten days' notice to pack up and leave their homes. They were ordered to bring only what they could carry themselves, including dishes, eating utensils, clothing, blankets, and bed linens for each family member. Tags with the family's registration number were attached to all luggage, and everyone had to wear a numbered tag on his or her clothes.

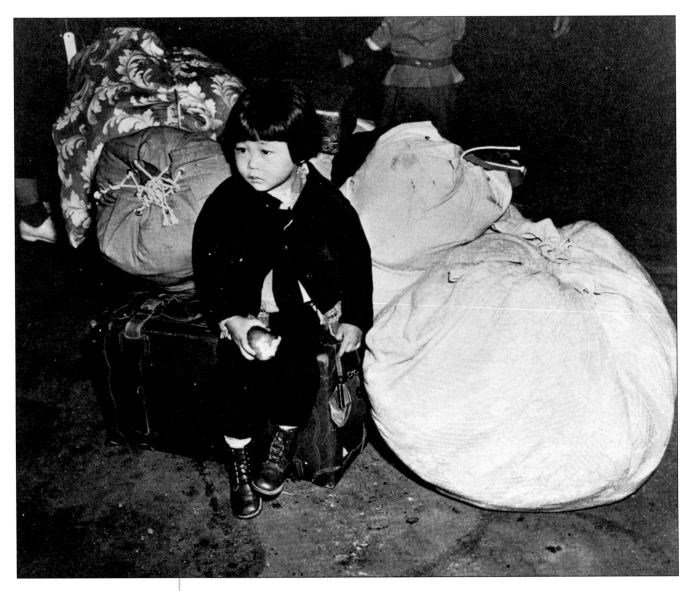

A little girl sits by her family's belongings and waits for transport.

People had to store or dispose of the rest of their belongings. Cars and furniture were often sold for far less than their actual worth. For many children the hardest task was leaving behind a beloved pet. Yoshiko Uchida cried over leaving her Scotch collie, Laddie, with a stranger.

TEMPORARY ASSEMBLY CENTERS

Japanese Americans were loaded onto buses or trains under the watch of military guards. They were taken to sixteen temporary detention camps that the government called assembly centers. Most of the assembly centers were racetracks or fairgrounds that were hastily converted into camps. Families lived in animal stalls or small windowless shacks.

The Uchida family was sent to Tanforan Racetrack in San Bruno, California, on May 1, 1942. They were assigned to **Barracks** 16, Apartment 40. The "barracks" was actually an

TANFORAN

Today, a shopping center is located on the site of the Tanforan Assembly Center in San Bruno, California.

Inside a barracks

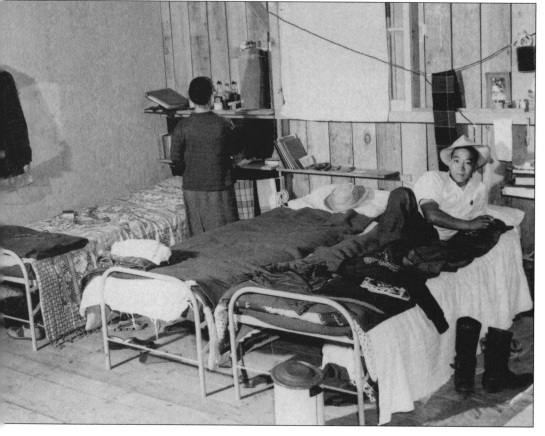

old horse stable, and the "apartment" was a dark horse stall, ten feet wide by twenty feet long. It was dirty and smelled of horse manure. The furnishings consisted of three metal army cots and a single bare light bulb dangling from the ceiling. The Uchida family lived there for the next five months.

Meals at assembly centers were served in **mess halls**. There were frequent shortages of food. Showers, toilets, and laundry facilities were in separate buildings. Laundry had to be washed by hand in large tubs. Most camps were surrounded with barbed wire fences and had guard towers with armed soldiers.

By early August, 120,000 Japanese Americans were removed from their homes on the West Coast and **interned,** or locked up, in detention camps. Loyal, law-abiding citizens had become prisoners of their own country.

Because of relocation and internment, many Japanese Americans lost their jobs, homes, and businesses. Their educations and careers were disrupted. Yoshiko Uchida missed attending her university graduation ceremony by two weeks. She received her college diploma by mail in her horse stall at Tanforan.

Japanese Americans suffered the humiliation of being imprisoned as suspected traitors in their own country. They lost their freedom and their constitutional rights. They also lost their innocent beliefs about what it meant to be an American.

Nevertheless, most Japanese Americans still felt a strong sense of loyalty to the United States. Yoshiko Uchida explained, "We had been raised to respect and trust those in authority. Resistance or confrontation such as we know them today was unthinkable, for the world then was a totally different place." Japanese Americans believed that cooperating with the government was the only way to prove their loyalty and help their country.

There was no mass relocation and internment in Hawaii, where the population was one-third Japanese American. It would have been impossible to transport that many people to the mainland, and the Hawaiian economy would have collapsed without Japanese American workers.

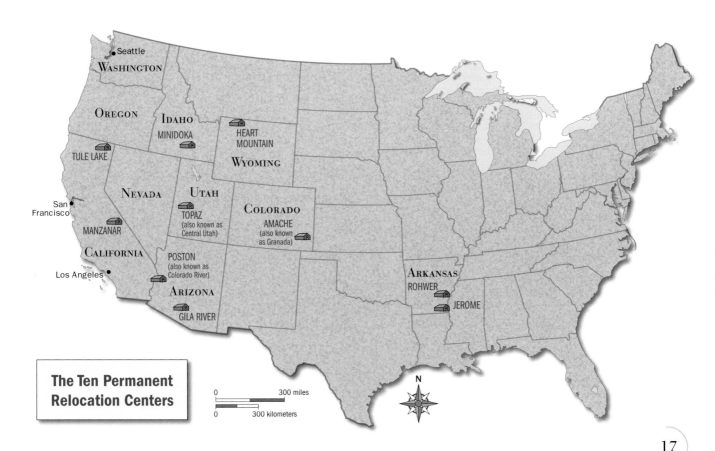

The Ten Permanent Relocation Centers

0   300 miles

0   300 kilometers

PERMANENT RELOCATION CENTERS

During the summer and fall of 1942 the **internees** were transferred from the temporary detention centers to ten permanent "relocation centers." The relocation centers were built and run by a new government agency called the War Relocation Authority, or the WRA. The permanent camps were scattered throughout the states of California,

Heart Mountain Relocation Center, Heart Mountain, Wyoming

Colorado, Wyoming, Idaho, Arizona, Utah, and Arkansas. Each camp held between eight thousand and twenty thousand people.

These camps were all located in isolated areas with extreme climates, such as deserts or swamps. Strong winds and blowing dust were common at many camps. Topaz, in the central Utah desert, had frequent, severe dust storms. Dust would seep through the cracks in the buildings' walls, covering everything with a thick layer of dirt.

Scorching summers were normal at many camps. At Gila River in Arizona, summer temperatures often reached a high of 125 degrees Fahrenheit (51.5°Celsius). Freezing winters were common in the northern camps. At Heart Mountain, Wyoming, winter temperatures often dipped to minus 30 degrees Fahrenheit (-34.5°C). The internees, used to the mild climate of the West Coast, found the extreme cold and heat difficult to bear.

Rohwer, in Arkansas, was built near swampland. The weather there was often very hot and humid. There were severe thunderstorms. George Takei was only four years old when he was sent to Rohwer with his parents, his little brother, and his baby sister. He spent most of his childhood behind barbed wire.

Each relocation center had its own administration building, school, hospital, camp store, and post office. The camps were designed in block arrangements.

CHILDREN'S VILLAGE

In June 1942, Japanese American children from orphanages in Los Angeles and San Francisco were sent to a special children's village at Camp Manzanar in California. One hundred and one children, most under seven years old, lived at the children's village until it closed in August 1945.

Each block contained a mess hall, a laundry building, bathrooms, and fourteen military-style barracks, or living quarters, where the families lived.

The barracks were made of wooden boards covered with tarpaper. The flimsy buildings did little to keep out summer heat or winter cold and wind. Fire was a constant threat in the wood-and-tarpaper communities.

Several families were crowded together into one building. A typical barracks was 120 feet long by 20 feet wide (37 meters by 6 meters). It was divided into 6 one-room "apartments" of various sizes. A family of five people would receive an apartment 24 feet long by 20 feet wide (7 m by 6 m). Each room was furnished with a wood-burning stove, one light fixture hanging from the ceiling, and a metal army cot for each person. Internees often made additional furniture from scraps of wood.

There was no plumbing in the barracks. People had to walk to other buildings to shower, use the toilet, or do laundry. Meals were eaten in mess halls, and residents had to wait in long lines for food. At first, there were shortages of food and other necessities. The daily food budget averaged 39 cents per person. Farms were started by internees to grow their own fruits and vegetables. Many also raised livestock, such as chickens, pigs, and cows.

In the barracks, only a thin wooden wall separated families from each other. They could hear everything their neighbors said. There was no privacy and nowhere to be alone. All mail was censored, and internees were not allowed to write or speak Japanese. Everything had to be in English so that camp authorities could monitor everything

A view of the block layout of a Japanese American Internment Camp

A TRUE FRIEND

Clara Breed was the children's librarian at the San Diego Public Library. She wrote letters and sent small gifts to many of the Japanese American children in the camps. Her kindness helped to keep their spirits up during their internment.

that was said. Head counts took place twice a day, and there were frequent searches for forbidden items, such as cameras and shortwave radios.

Most camps were surrounded by barbed-wire fences and guard towers. Armed guards were instructed to shoot anyone trying to leave. However, there were no guards at Jerome, Arkansas. Swamps with four species of poisonous snakes surrounded that camp.

Guards look over an internment camp.

Nursery school children draw
pictures and make cut-outs at
Tule Lake Segregation Center.

The residents did their best to form a community. They established schools and churches, and each camp started its own community newspaper. Boy Scout and Girl Scout troops were important activities for the youngsters, and adults joined art classes and hobby groups. People of all ages enjoyed playing and watching sports such as baseball, basketball, and judo.

★ ★ ★ ★

The mess hall was the social center of camp life. Meetings, dances, concerts, and talent shows were held there. Movies were frequently shown in the evenings. At Poston, movies were shown outdoors, and people had to bring their own chairs.

Although books and supplies were scarce, schools held classes, PTA meetings, open houses, and other normal school activities. The high schools had student council elections and graduation ceremonies, complete with caps

Japanese American internees weed onions at Tule Lake Segregation Center

and gowns. Yoshiko Uchida wrote, ". . . the children wanted to be in school. They were longing for a normal routine and needed school to give them the sense of security and order that had been snatched from them so abruptly."

Adults often found jobs inside the camps. Internees grew fruits and vegetables on the farm, wrote for the community newspaper, or worked at the camp store. Those who were trained nurses and doctors worked in the hospital. Yoshiko Uchida taught second grade in the school at Topaz.

Japanese American workers received between $16 and $21 a month, while non-Japanese workers who were brought in to fill labor shortages were paid much higher salaries. At Topaz, Yoshiko Uchida received $19 a month. Non-Japanese teachers hired by the WRA were paid between $150 and $200 a month. Japanese American doctors at Heart Mountain Hospital made $19 to $21 a month, while non-Japanese nurses at the same hospital made $150 a month.

Internees often left the camps on temporary work leaves. With so many Americans away fighting the war, there was a labor shortage in many industries. Farmers needed workers to harvest their crops, and many Japanese Americans were experienced farmers. Some of them picked sugar beets in Utah, some harvested potatoes in Idaho. Others worked at the vegetable canneries in Salt Lake City. These temporary work assignments were a welcome break from the camps and a chance to earn extra money. Outside jobs paid far more than internees earned in camp.

MILITARY SERVICE

Immediately after Pearl Harbor five thousand Japanese Americans serving in the United States military were discharged or transferred to non-combat units. They were considered unfit for military duty because of their ancestry.

Japanese American soldiers during World War II

The decorated members
of the Japanese American
100th Infantry

In June 1942 the army decided to test the loyalty and combat ability of Japanese Americans by forming the 100th
Infantry Battalion, a unit composed almost entirely of Japanese Americans from Hawaii. The 100th Infantry Battalion
performed so well during training that the government
opened military service to all Japanese Americans. A new
all–Japanese American unit, the 442nd Regimental Combat Team, accepted volunteers from both the mainland
and Hawaii. Nearly one thousand men from Hawaii,
including Daniel Inouye, volunteered the first day.

The soldiers of the 442ⁿᵈ Regimental Combat Team at a dance

President Roosevelt announced the decision to accept Japanese American volunteers on February 1, 1943. He stated, "No loyal citizen of the United States should be denied the democratic right to exercise the responsibilities of his citizenship, regardless of his ancestry. . . . Americanism is not, and never was, a matter of race or ancestry." Many Japanese Americans found this statement bitterly ironic, since they had been interned solely because of their race and ancestry.

* * * *

GO FOR BROKE!

GO FOR BROKE!

The motto of the 100th Infantry Battalion/442nd Regimental Combat Team was "Go for Broke!" Daniel Inouye said, "It meant giving everything we had . . . scrambling over an obstacle course as though our lives depended on it; marching quick time until we were ready to drop."

Nevertheless, more than twelve hundred internees volunteered. They saw it as an opportunity to demonstrate the loyalty and courage of Japanese Americans in a dramatic and forceful way.

In June 1944 the 100th Infantry Battalion became part of the 442nd Regimental Combat Team. The combined 100th Infantry Battalion/442nd Regimental Combat Team fought in eight major battles in Europe. It received more awards than any other unit in American military history. It earned 18,143 medals for courage and 9,486 Order of the Purple Heart awards, given to soldiers wounded in action. Second Lieutenant Daniel Inouye received a Purple Heart, a Bronze Star, a Distinguished Service Cross, and twelve other medals for bravery. Unfortunately, he lost his right arm from a German grenade exploding at close range.

The Purple Heart medal

29

★ ★ ★ ★

LOYALTY QUESTIONNAIRE

In February 1943 the government decided that all adult internees should answer a loyalty questionnaire. Questions twenty-seven and twenty-eight were the most important. Question twenty-seven asked if internees were willing to serve in the U.S. military. Question twenty-eight asked them to swear allegiance to the United States and to **forswear,** or give up, any loyalty to Japan. American citizens wondered how they could give up a loyalty they had never felt. They

The remains of Tule Lake Segregation Center in Newell, California

worried that this question was an attempt to trick them into saying that they were not loyal Americans. Internees who were still citizens of Japan also worried. The U.S. government would not allow them to become American citizens. If they gave up their Japanese citizenship, they would be people without a country.

Internees who answered no to both questions were considered disloyal. The 8,500 "disloyals" and their families were sent to Tule Lake Segregation Center, a maximum-security camp in northern California. Half the 18,000 residents at Tule Lake were children, including George Takei. His parents had answered no to both questions.

Mrs. Takei and more than five thousand other Japanese Americans became so bitter about their internment that they **renounced,** or gave up, their U.S. citizenship. Later, most of them regretted that decision. It took years of lawsuits and legal appeals before their American citizenship was restored.

A Japanese American back at work. Behind him is a sign advertising U.S. Savings Bonds and stamps that were sold to help fund the war effort.

LEAVING THE CAMPS

The War Relocation Authority encouraged "loyal" Japanese Americans to leave the internment camps permanently if they could find jobs in the Midwest or East. They were not allowed to return to the restricted area on the West Coast.

College students were also allowed to leave if they could find schools willing to accept them. About 5,500 students took advantage of this opportunity. The National Japanese American Student Relocation Council was a private organization that helped Yoshiko Uchida and thousands of other college students leave the camps and return to school.

★ ★ ★ ★

The internees tried hard to stay busy and live as normally as possible under the circumstances. But it was difficult not to feel despair and depression. Yoshiko Uchida wrote, "The **bleakness** of Topaz was now seeping deep inside me. . . . I felt as though I couldn't bear being locked up one more day. I wanted to go out into the world and live a real life."

Yoshiko Uchida filled out official forms, wrote letters, and waited many months before receiving permission to leave Topaz in May 1943. She enrolled as a graduate student at Smith College in Massachusetts. Her sister Keiko also received permission to leave and accepted a job as a nursery school assistant at Mt. Holyoke College in Massachusetts.

The sisters were overjoyed to leave Topaz and to live so near each other. However, they were sad to leave their parents imprisoned behind barbed wire. Yoshiko Uchida received her master's degree in education from Smith College in May 1944. Then she found a job teaching first and second grades at a small Quaker school in Philadelphia.

A seven-year-old boy rides his bike through the abandoned streets of Tule Lake Segregation Center in Newell, California.

RETURNING HOME

In December 1944, President Roosevelt announced that the internment camps would close by the end of 1945. Japanese Americans were allowed to return to the West Coast beginning January 2, 1945. Internees were given a train ticket and $25. Many Japanese Americans had no

Japanese Americans Kim Yamasaki and Albert Nozaki, designing engineers, out of the camps and back to work

The Manzanar National Historic Site

homes or jobs to return to. Some moved to the Midwest and East, but most went back to the West Coast.

All Japanese Americans faced years of struggle and hardship to start life over. Often people found that their stored belongings were stolen or damaged. Jobs and housing were scarce, and many families ended up living in trailer parks for returning internees.

MANZANAR PILGRIMAGE

Every year on the last Saturday of April, former internees make a pilgrimage, or journey, to Manzanar National Historic Site in California. The Manzanar Pilgrimage commemorates the closing of the internment camps.

35

A mushroom cloud rises over Nagasaki from the atomic bomb explosion, August 9, 1945.

* * * *

On August 6, 1945, the United States dropped an atomic bomb on the Japanese city of Hiroshima. Three days later a second atomic bomb was dropped, this one on Nagasaki. Japan surrendered on August 14, 1945.

Prejudice against Japanese Americans did not end with the war. Daniel Inouye spent twenty months in military hospitals recovering from his war wounds. Later, when he walked into a barbershop in San Francisco, the barber told him, "You're a Jap, and we don't cut Jap hair."

Senator Daniel Inouye, August 4, 1964

37

Daniel Inouye recalled, "There I stood, in full uniform, the new captain's bars bright on my shoulder, four rows of ribbons on my chest, the combat infantry badge, the distinguished unit citations—and a hook where my hand was supposed to be. And he didn't cut Jap hair. To think that I had gone through a war to save his skin—and he didn't cut Jap hair."

Daniel Inouye did not let prejudice or the loss of his arm defeat him. He graduated from the University of Hawaii, and in 1952 he received a law degree from George Washington University in Washington, D.C. That same year a law was passed that finally gave Japanese immigrants, like Daniel Inouye's father, the right to become American citizens. On August 21, 1959, Hawaii became the fiftieth state of the United States, and Daniel Inouye became the new state's first U.S. congressman and the first Japanese American elected to Congress. In 1962 he was elected to represent Hawaii in the U.S. Senate.

Yoshiko Uchida became an award-winning author of children's books. Several of her books, including *Journey to Topaz* and *Journey Home,* deal with her experiences during her internment and her life afterward.

George Takei earned both a bachelor of arts and a master of arts in theater from the University of California at Los Angeles. He became a professional actor. Although he has appeared in dozens of movies and television shows, he is best known for his role as Mr. Sulu in the popular *Star Trek* television series and movies. George Takei is also a community activist. He serves on the board of governors of East West Players, the country's leading Asian Pacific

American theater, and he is a member of the Japan–United States Friendship Commission. In 2000 he became chairman of the Board of the Japanese American National Museum.

Actor George Takei

CORRECTING INJUSTICES

In 1980, Senator Daniel Inouye of Hawaii cosponsored a bill creating the Commission on Wartime Relocation and Internment of Civilians, or CWRIC. The CWRIC's task was to investigate the relocation and internment and report its findings to Congress. In 1981 the CWRIC held hearings in six cities across the country. Seven hundred and fifty witnesses, including George Takei, testified about their wartime internment.

On June 23, 1983, the CWRIC concluded that the relocation and internment "were not justified by military necessity, and the decisions to do so were based on racial prejudice, war hysteria, and a failure of political leadership." The CWRIC recommended that the president offer a national apology to Japanese Americans and that the nation pay $20,000 to each surviving internee. These recommendations became law on August 10, 1988, when President Ronald Reagan signed the Civil Liberties Act of 1988. On October 9, 1990, 107-year-old Reverend Mamoru Eto of Los Angeles was the first person to receive a check for twenty thousand dollars. Eventually, a total of 82,219 individuals received payments.

Another wartime injustice was corrected at a White House ceremony on June 21, 2000. Daniel Inouye and nineteen other Japanese Americans were awarded the Medal of Honor, the nation's highest military award, for their courage during World War II. Previously, only one Japanese American had ever received the Medal of Honor.

"There was concern that wartime conditions—the bitter feelings about Pearl Harbor and the suspicion of all Japanese Americans—had prevented Japanese American soldiers who made extraordinary contributions in combat from being properly recognized," U.S. Secretary of the Army Louis Caldera said. "This recognition for many Japanese Americans helps wipe away much of the **stigma** that was associated with those wartime suspicions and it helps set the record straight for all time."

The wartime internment of Japanese Americans is a dark chapter in our country's history. As Yoshiko Uchida said, all Americans must "be **vigilant,** so that such a tragedy will never happen to any group of people in America ever again."

Kaun Onodera, a veteran who fought with the 442nd Infantry Regiment, shows the Bronze Star he earned in World War II.

Glossary

aliens—people who are not citizens of the country in which they live; foreigners

ammunition—explosive material used for weapons

ancestry—people, ethnic group, or country from which one is descended

barracks—building where soldiers live; large, plain building used for temporary living quarters

bleakness—gloominess; dreariness; barrenness

forswear—to deny or give up under oath

hysteria—very strong fear or panic

interned—locked up or confined

internees—people locked up or confined

mess halls—places where food is cooked and served

relocation—movement from one place to another

renounced—gave up or disowned by formal
 announcement

stigma—mark of shame or disgrace

treason—betrayal of one's country by helping an enemy

vigilant—watchful; on the alert

Timeline: Japanese

1939 - 1945	1941	1942	1942	1943	1945	1952

World War II is fought

DECEMBER 7
Japan attacks Pearl Harbor

DECEMBER 8
United States declares war on Japan

FEBRUARY 19
Executive Order 9066 authorizes removal of Japanese Americans from West Coast

MARCH 18
War Relocation Authority created to run internment camps

JUNE
100th Infantry Battalion, composed almost entirely of Japanese Americans from Hawaii, is formed

DAILY NEWS   FINAL

JAPAN AT WAR WITH U.S.

Hawaii, Philippines And Guam Bombed

FLEET HITS BACK

FEBRUARY
All adult internees forced to answer loyalty questionnaire

JANUARY 2
Internees allowed to return to West Coast

AUGUST 14
Japan surrenders; World War II ends

JUNE 27
Japanese immigrants gain right to become U.S. citizens

American Internment

1980	1983	1988	1990
JULY 31 Commission on Wartime Relocation and Internment of Civilians (CWRIC) formed	**JUNE 23** CWRIC recommends apology and $20,000 payment per internee	**AUGUST 10** Civil Liberties Act of 1988 provides for apology and $20,000 payments to former internees	

OCTOBER 9 First $20,000 payment made

To Find Out More

BOOKS

Stanley, Jerry. *I Am an American.* New York: Crown Publishers, 1994.

Tunnell, Michael O., and George W. Chilcoat. *The Children of Topaz.* New York: Holiday House, 1996.

Uchida, Yoshiko. *Journey Home.* New York: Aladdin Books, 1992.

Uchida, Yoshiko. *Journey to Topaz.* Berkeley, CA: Creative Arts, 1985.

ONLINE SITES

Japanese American National Museum
http://www.janm.org/

Manzanar National Historic Site
http://www.nps.gov/manz/

National Japanese American Historical Society
http://www.nikkeiheritage.org/

Index

Bold numbers indicate illustrations.

About the Author

Gail Sakurai is the author of numerous nonfiction books for young readers. She specializes in writing biographies of famous people and books about American history. Some of her most recent books include *Asian-Americans in the Old West, The Thirteen Colonies,* and *Juan Ponce de León.* Ms. Sakurai is a member of the Society of Children's Book Writers and Illustrators. She lives in Cincinnati, Ohio, with her husband and two sons. When she is not researching or writing, she enjoys traveling with her family and visiting America's historical sites.